My First
BUG
PICTURE BOOK

LEARN ABOUT BUGS

30 FUN & INTERESTING FACTS

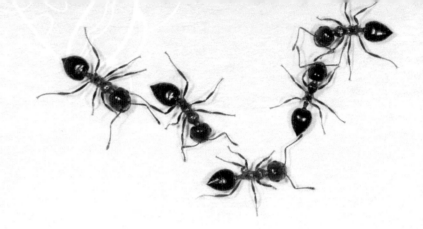

Paperback Edition: 9781960320247
Hardcover Edition: 9781960320254
Digital Edition: 9781960320261

Published in the United States by Two Ravens Books LLC,
254 Chapman Rd, Ste 209, Newark DE 19702

'Expand the mind, free the imagination, one title at a time.'
www.tworavensbooks.com

Two Little Ravens
CHILDREN'S NON-FICTION BOOKS

Bugs!

A ladybug might change color when it dies.

Spooky, but true!

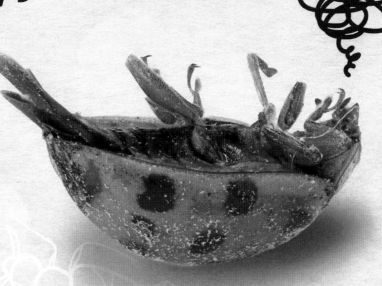

Crickets hear through their **knees.**

Now, that's knee-slapping funny!

You can tell a cricket's temperature by listening to its chirp.

Grasshoppers have ears on their bellies.

Tummy tunes, anyone?

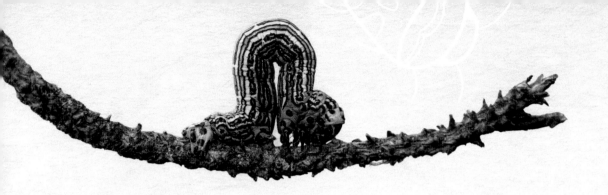

Caterpillars have 12 eyes. That's a lot of eye exams!

Caterpillars have more muscles than humans.

They have about 4,000!

A single ant colony can have up to 50 million members.

That's a big family!

Ants don't have ears, and they use their feet to hear by feeling vibrations.

Some ants are lazy, and they don't do any work and just hang around.

Some ants can EXPLODE.

Don't worry; they only do it to protect their friends.

Some ants farm aphids for their honeydew.

They're tiny bug farmers!

The loudest insect is the male cicada.

It's louder than a Rock Concert!

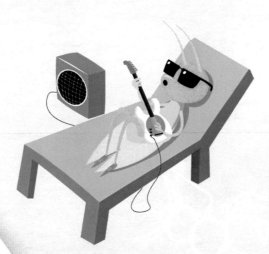

Bees have five eyes, but they can't see the color **RED**.

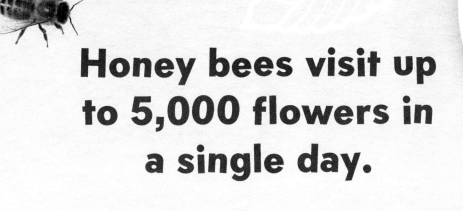

Honey bees visit up
to 5,000 flowers in
a single day.

They're super
busy bees!

A snail can sleep for three years.

Imagine that, three years of slumber parties!

Spiders aren't insects; they're arachnids with eight legs.

Spiders recycle their old webs by eating them.

Yum, silk soup!

A tarantula can go without food for more than two years.

They'd miss a lot of meals!

Dragonflies are super fast flyers. They can zip around at 35 miles per hour.

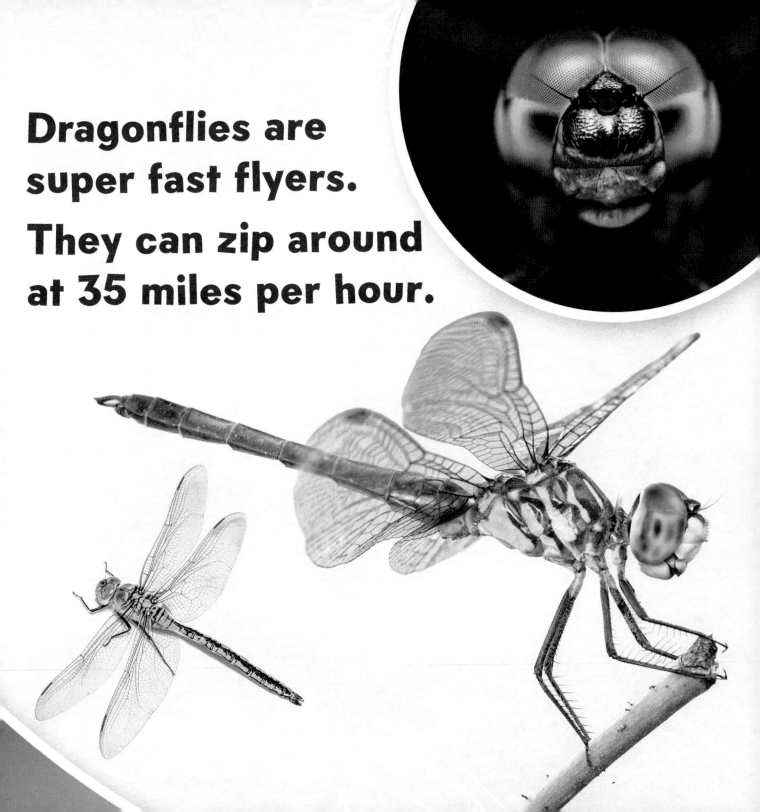

Fireflies aren't flies; they're beetles that glow in the dark.

Firefly lights can be yellow, green, or red.

They're living Christmas lights!

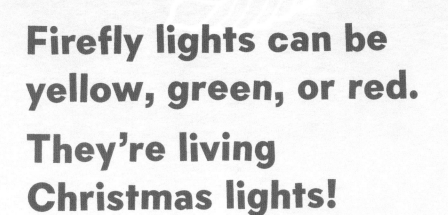

Dung Beetles love to roll in poop.

Icky, but true!

Butterflies can't fly if they're too cold.

They need to warm up their wings first.

Butterflies taste with their feet.

Now that's a weird dinner party!

A butterfly that looks like an owl is called the

Owl Butterfly.

Some beetles can change color.

They're like little bug chameleons!

Some beetles look
like army tanks.

They're called
tortoise beetles.

The Goliath Beetle
is as heavy as
a hamster.

A bug-sized pet!

Praying Mantis can turn its head around like an owl.

Super swivel head!

Silk comes from silkworms, and they spin it for their cocoons.

There's a bug that looks like a leaf.

It's the Leaf Insect!

TWORAVENS
B O O K S

Collectible imprints
for little learners & readers

Xander & Rem
Children's Coloring & Activity Books

Xander's Perch
CHILDREN'S FICTION BOOKS

Two Little Ravens
CHILDREN'S NON-FICTION BOOKS

Hello Brilliant Little Reader and Grown-Up Guide!

Thanks for embarking on the fun-filled educational journey in this book.

We hope you chuckled your way through each page, learning and laughing in equal measure.

If you have ideas to make this book more helpful for you and others, don't hesitate to email us at **hello@tworavensbooks.com.**

If your funny bone was tickled and your brain ignited by this adventure, we'd be delighted if you could share your giggles and gains by reviewing **My First Bug Picture Book.**

Your feedback not only helps others find this book but also fuels us to keep weaving humor and knowledge into more wonderful titles.

Keep laughing, keep learning, and thank you for your support of **Two Little Ravens**, an imprint of **Two Ravens Books LLC.**

Find more humorously educational books like this at **TwoRavensBooks.com.**

Made in the USA
Las Vegas, NV
01 July 2023

74107853R00031